RHYTHM

IN

MY

WORDS

ISBN: 1-4140-0249-1 (e-book)
ISBN: 1-4140-0248-3 (Paperback)

Library of Congress Control Number: 2003098026

This book is printed on acid free paper.

Printed in the United States of America
Bloomington, IN

1stBooks – rev. 12/23/03

May this book be as joyful for your reading, as it was for my writing.   Truly God has blessed me with a poetic gift and it is my sincere desire to share His gift with you.

I pray that heaven will continue to shine upon you and yours. Poetically yours, simply rita.

P.s. remember, a dream is not dead, just dormant, waiting for you to awake and rise to the occasion.

In Loving Memory of my
Grandmother
Ms. Maderia Bell Jernigan

Given To This Earth: 8-24-20

Departed From Us: 3-13-03

TABLE OF CONTENTES

ABOUT THE AUTHOR

simply rita is new to the publishing world, however, she's a veteran in her craft. At the age of eight she discovered her ability to put words together in a rhythmic pattern, however, it would be twenty years before her gift would be introduced to the world.

simply rita sampled her work in her hometown of Muncie Indiana by way of calendars, greeting cards, and poetry recitals. With the encouragement of family and friends and her strong spiritual beliefs, simply rita decided to live her dream of becoming an author.

Simply rita is also looking forward to publishing her second children's story, as well as, releasing her 2004 poetry calendar.

Without fail, I give all glory and honor to God for His gift, blessings, mercy, and grace. Truly without Him, this book could not have come to pass.

To my husband, Cliff, for his unending love, support, and prayers for me and my dreams, truly you are my earthly angel.

To my children, Josh and Tiffany, you're more of an inspiration than you'll ever know. Always remember, that mommy loves you.

To my family and friends, you asked about it for years, now here it is. I pray your anticipation was not in vain.
Rhythmically yours,
simply rita

COME

Come join me in the reading of
The poems from my heart
The gift of rhythm in the words
All poets know the part

Come join me in the melody
That comes from every verse
Embrace the chance to have a dance
With steps so unrehearsed

I have a phrase prepared for you
To take away your gloom
Dim the lights prepare to glide
Across my dancing room

Come join me in the reading of
Some words to comfort true
Release your mind and you will find
This rhythm is for you

WHAT IF

What if I listen instead of talking?
Then you'd hear all I want you to hear.

What if I respond in love rather than anger?
Then love would turn my wrath.

What if I asked instead of demand?
Then you'd get from me all and more.

What if I try instead of quitting?
Then I would show you the way.

What if I give instead of take?
Then you'd bless and be blessed.

What if I help instead of hinder?
Then I'll stop all who hinders you.

What if I pray instead of complaining?
Then I'd answer again and again

CHANCE

A heart that does not learn to love
Is a heart that does not live
A soul that does not have a gift
Is a soul that cannot give

A mind that does not learn to soar
As eagles in the sky
Is trapped and it will never know
To where the eagles fly

The one who will not dare to dream
Is one who will not chance
The one who will not play a song
Is one who will not dance

The one who will not dare to read
Will never know old times
Like Edgar Allen or Shakespeare
The poets and their rhymes

The one who has a mansion high
But lives in just one room
Will be a rose before its time
And therefore will not bloom

The one who chances, gives, and dreams
Is destine to be free
To live, to have, to hold, to live
Out every fantasy

TO

To touch
Is to feel

To feel
Is to know

To know
Is to live

A lifetime of love

ME

Look at Me
I want to see
Reflections of
The greatest love
Oh please
Look at me

Reach for me
I want to be
Embraced upon
From dust to dawn
Do please
Reach for me

Cleave to me
And never flee
For love is rare
And if you dare
Cleave
Cleave to me

Love is free
For you and me
It's free for you and me

WHERE

Where are the homes for homeless ones
The shelters for the old
Is out of reach the hope of change
To shield them from the cold

Where is the help for fellow men
For women and their young
Is gone for good a helping hand
How did this world become

The bitter from the sweetest sweet
The sour through and through
The roughness with a jagged edge
Uncaring of the view

Where is the hope for happiness
The chance, the help, the dream
The something out of nothings start
The captain and his team

I pray that we would see ahead
The danger of our course
I plead for us to turn around
Be kind and show remorse

I charge for us to take a stand
Demand for all to own
The comforts and the daily needs
A house that is a home

Where are the homes for homeless ones
Let's build if that's the case
Let's lend a hand to every man
And shame will be erased

YOUR LOVE

In my life time
Some doors have slammed
Some glass has shattered
And this heart's been broken

Many times I was told
You get the ups with the downs
The good with the bad
And the bitter with the sweet

True into each life
Some rain must fall
A sigh must be made
And a tear or two must drop

But now that I have you
There's cushioned arms
To lift me up
And catch me when I fall

I find in you pure cane
Occasionally some sweet and low
Fewer calories never hurt anyone
But still we are always equal

So maybe a door may slam
Or a glass or two might shatter
But when this heart is broken
Your love mends it back together.

A ROSE GREW

A rose grew in my yard today
And I adored the sight
I had to bend and smell the gift
Which made my yard so bright
A rose grew in my yard today
And it was plain to see
That it was sent to show the love
That God feels so for me

A ROSE GREW

THE SEA

When I was lost
Confused inside
It seemed so hard
To find a guide
But then came you
My heart was fast
I said within
Relief at last

We crossed the beach
We swam the sea
And I felt love
From you to me
My heart grew big
I thought for sure
That at this time
Love would endure

But out burst thunder
Down came rain
A bolt of lightening
A stroke of pain
And you are gone
Oh damn the sea
For drowning you
And leaving me

YOUR SPIRIT

You bring out the best in me, by putting the best into me, and that would be your spirit!

I DREAMED OF YOU

I dreamed of you last night
and it was a dream of sweet splendor, and essence, as the
thought of loving you lingered in my mind.

I dreamed of you last night, but a dream is just that, and not
reality, so I begged the moon to go away and find for me
the sun, for the sun, and none other compares to the
brightness you bestow into my life, and the night, though
brilliant with stars can only bring back to me an illusion.

True, I live to relive the memories of you and I in a day, but
it's a hallucination, thus turning my sweet dream into a
bitter sorrow.

Leak a tear brown eyes of mine, but let it be tears of joy, for
in the morning it comes and with it is you.

I dreamed of you last night
Ever sweet
Ever tender
I dreamed of you.

AGAINST

Against the norm, against the grain
Against the greatest odds
I made it through the toughest times
I know because of God

Against the downs and turn a rounds
Against the strongest wind
I gave it up I prayed it up
I let it go again

The turning through the winter nights
The hurting through the storm
The crying as a heavy rain
For me was not the norm

Yet such is life, the good and bad
The bitter with the sweet
A yes and no will come and go
And trick instead of treat

But through it all, my greatest fall
My deepest depth of pain
It showed the glory of the Lord
His strength helped me sustain

Against the norm against the grain
I know it to be true
No matter what the odds may be
I know He'll pull me through

R.O.S.E.

R.
Reach me with your beauty

O
Open me with your fragrance

S
Surrender me with your sweetness

E
Embrace me with your petals

DEPOSIT

You have deposited so much
Into me
And the beauty of your
Bank is that
My account is never
Overdrawn

IN YOU

In you I see the rising sun
That settles at days end
In you I see the shining moon
Which lets romance begin
In you I have the world at hand
To give all that I need
In you I have to ask but once
And it is mine's in deed
From you I have the very thing
My heart needs to endure
And I embrace it very tight
To keep this love secure
Unlike the ships passed in the night
And never loved again
We two are forever more
Our love from deep within
In you I find no need to search
For truly I have found
A love that is forever mine
Together we are bound
My heart, my love, my everything,
My love forever true
You have given much to me
I've found it all in you

A KISS

My wake up
My get up
My go

A kiss

My comfort
My tingle
My glow

A kiss

Affection
Emotion
Galore

A Kiss

Excitement
Enlighten
And more

A kiss

It's all found in a kiss

TOMORROW

I WON'T SAY I LOVE YOU 'TIL THE END OF
TIME
FOR THAT WOULD SUGGEST AN END
TO SOMETHING THAT'S ENDLESS
AND PUT BOUNDARIES ON SOMETHING
THAT'S BOUNDLESS

'CAUSE LIMITS ARE FOR THOSE UNDER
CONTROL
BUT AS FOR US THERE ARE NO
RESTRAINTS,
NO DO NOT'S, WILL NOT'S, OR CANT'S
JUST YES FOREVER AND ALWAYS

I LOVED YOU SO MUCH YESTERDAY
I'M EVER IN LOVE WITH YOU TODAY
AND TOMORROW, MY LOVE, WILL FIND
ME
STILL ETERNALLY LOVING YOU

SIMPLY SAY

So simple the phrase
Which brightens our days
And yet I'm compelled
To share what is held
In side of me
As pure as can be

I love you

NIGHT THOUGHTS

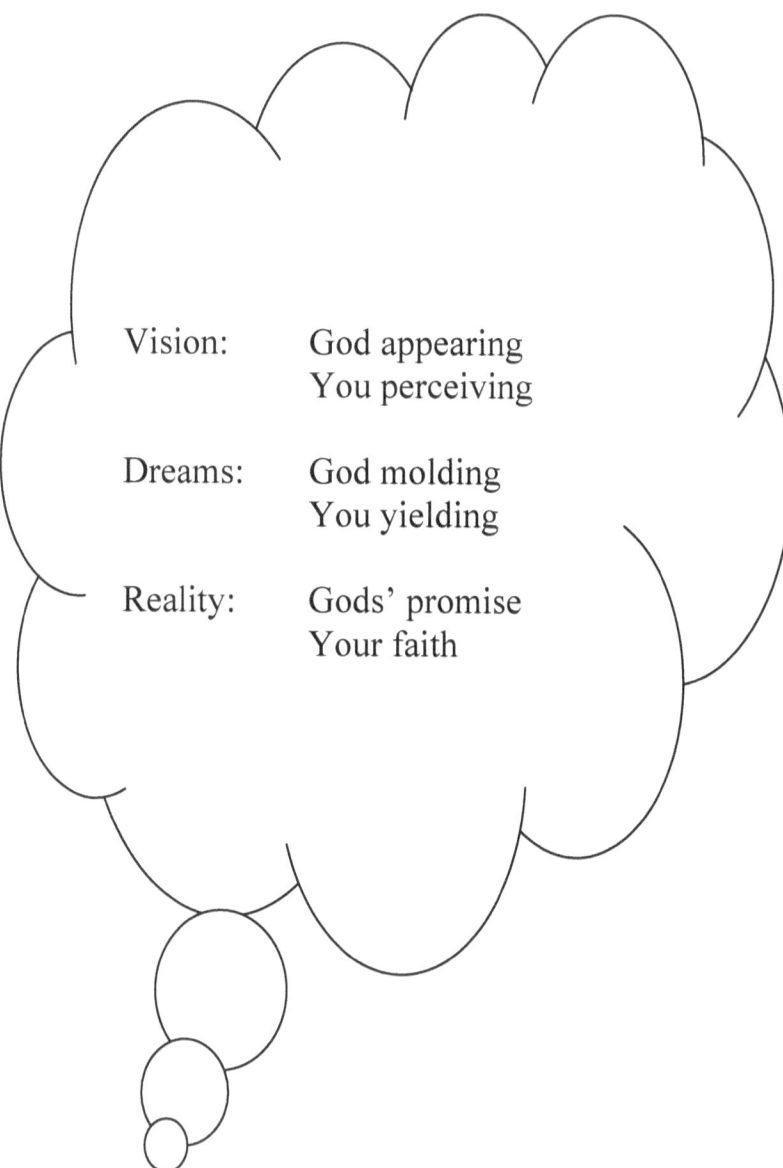

Vision: God appearing
             You perceiving

Dreams: God molding
             You yielding

Reality: Gods' promise
             Your faith

ANOTHER YEAR

What have I done to find myself
Approaching one more year
What grace is given unto me
Who grants me to be here?

What have I done, whom have I shown
A token of my love
When did I drive that extra mile
And did it just because

I do not know if I deserve
To see another day
Another week, another month
But to the Lord I say

For every year you've given me
For every bless'ed season
I know you have a greater plan
Though I know not the reason

And as I sit within my thoughts
Surrounded so by you
Not knowing what will
Come to pass
But knowing that you do

I pray I'm worthy of your grace
Your mercy one by one
But then again, I say I am
Because you gave your Son.

WHY

Why should I wait for the sun, the
moon or the stars, for you're much
warmer, closer, and brighter

FRIENDSHIP

Not for fame or fortune have I befriended thee, but just because you're you

QUOETICALLY

Quoetically, poetically
The thoughts within my mind
A ray of hope, a soothing glance
Like that of olden times

Poetically, quoetically
Confucius had his say
Now quotes beyond the distance past
Must yield unto today

So true the words I give to you
So simple in its verse
The best from me, philosophy
Is pure and unrehearsed

And yet I share a meaning deep
With words so clear and true
Intriguing for the brilliant mind
Uplifting through and through

Quoetically, poetically
No need to be surprised
I have for you, a quote or two
My wisdom to the wise

IN A WORLD

In a world so large and cold
It's good to know one thing
That I am loved so much by you
Oh, the joy you bring

In a world so dark with lust
So sinful and so cruel
It's good to know that I have you
The exception to the rule

For it's not often one can find
The patience that you store
The love that never seems to end
Always an open door

And in this world forever great
It's hard for me to know
That if fate would change the road
I'd have no where to go

So let me cherish you right now
For 'morrow may not be
Let me hold forever close
The love that's dear to me

RESERVATIONS

Reservations with my love
A meal for us to share
A bite or two just me and you
The fragrance in the air

Radiates and wraps around
The table where we are
The holding eyes without goodbyes
My love and shining star

Candles to reflect the warmth
Which burns forever deep
Glasses to recite a toast
The love we plan to keep

Dinnerware to serve the food
To nourish us within
Followed by a sweet dessert
Reminding us again

That we are blessed to have the chance
To love out of the heart
To be embraced from day to day
We play a special part

And when we go back to the world
Of work and other things
May we look upon the noon
Such happiness it brings

Reservations with my love
Cuisines of master chefs
Linger on the palate of
A love that is the best

A SUPER BOWL WISH

Now I lay me
Down to sleep
I pray the Colts
Will win this week
I wish I may
I wish I might
For them to win
This Monday night
Oh happy, happy
I will be
If they will win
One game for me
I'll plan and plan
On nightly strolls
To help them win
Some Super Bowls
But just my luck
Without a care
They'll prove they do not
Have a prayer
But I believe
One day they can
Satisfy
Their only fan
And who knows
Perhaps some way
The Colts will win
A Bowl someday

MY STAR

Shining
Truly my bright spot

Tender
Ever soft is your touch

Amazing
You never fail to surprise

Rare
No jewel can compare

IN MY EYES

In my eyes you are the world
You are the moon and sun
In my eyes you are my pearls
I treasure everyone

In my heart you are the air
That breathes inside my soul
And in my mind I see you there
Your love as rich as coal

Though in this life there is dismay
So full of pain and fears
I can cry and it's o.k.
Your hand can dry my tears

My eyes, my heart, my mind, my life
Oh, the joy you bring
With you there is no longer strife
You are my everything

LOVE

Love is a planted seed
    That grows into a rose
        And is given as a gift

The rose will open a heart
    That closed because of pain
        And reopened because of love

Should the heart close again
    It's because the love has died
        The rose was not enhanced

So nurture the seed of love
    Inhale the sent of the rose
        Embrace the gift of love

HERE

Here I sit, this quiet place
It helps me drift away
Here I rock a steady pace
Don't even want to play
Here I sit to have my rest
And here I'll have my fun
I'm relaxed and at my best
For all my work is done

Here up high I hear a bird
That's singing in the tree
Please right now, don't say a word
Just let this bird sing free
Here I sit, this quiet place
Puts all my fears behind
For finally it's peace I face
And life is so sublime.

C.H.R.I.S.T.I.A.N.S.

Christians   Cares for you

Helps you through

Christians   Relieves your stress

Inspires the best

Christians   Share your pain

Teaches restrain

Christians   Insists you call

Answers all

Christians   Never quit

So this is it

IT'S WHAT CHRISTIANS DO

WINTER

If winter never came to be
We would not have the spring
The flowers would not be in bloom
The birds they would not sing

If winter never came to be
The earth it could not rest
The grass could never dare to grow
The greenest blades, the best

And so it is the way of life
The winter, it must come
The cold, the wind, the tears again
For each and everyone

But then the summer from the spring
The warmth, the breeze, and fall
Will come as it was meant to do
To soothe the pain and all

So winter have your season now
I'll weather all the snow
For spring is just a time away
And sorrow soon will go

PROTECTION

My cloud is not a symbol of sorrow, but rather the blanket of the Lord, protecting me during my storm

HEALER

Though the truth you speak may cut, you also give the antibiotic to heal, and the bandages to conceal from those waiting to penetrate my wound.

TRUTH

I've asked the Lord for many things
Much more than I can count
I've named the date I want it by
And even set amounts

For it is written in His word
I've read it, every part
"Delight yourself and you shall have
Desires of your heart."

But there's a problem with my choice
The error in my task
Was wanting only fleshly things
So selfishly, I asked

I never thought about the poor
When praying to the Lord
Everything was me and mine
So wholly self-absorbed

And never did I give a thought
Unto the homeless one
The sick the weak, so much defeat
Compassion, I had none

I dare to say it's not the way
To represent the King
To heaven sent, a deep repent
For all the sinful things

The olden one a sinful one
A fact I can't refute
But graciously a change in me
It's all because of truth

YOUR EYES

They pierce me
Soothe me
Move me

Your eyes

They warm me
Hold me
Show me

Your eyes

Touch me
Feel me
Heal me

Your eyes

I see it in your eyes

I FOUND

I did not find a
pot of gold

At the end of
the rainbow

Yet, something
better,

I found you

At times

At times you
may be alone,
but you need
never be lonely,
for I am a
thought, a dial,
or a drive away

I PROMISE

I promise to love you
As long as there is
Breath in my body
I promise to love you.

As long as our hearts
Cling together as one
I promise to love you

'Til the moonlight sets
And the sun rises again
I promise to love you

And when our love
Touch the end of the universe
And come back again
I will still love you

For in you
I find that our love
Can never end
I promise

SOMETIMES

Sometimes when I say I love you
I wonder if you really hear what
I'm saying, if you know what I'm
felling, or if you see that I care.

You seem to take my love for
granted as if you know I'll always
be here for you.

But just when I'm overwhelmed
with frustration, you overwhelm
me with your love, and it's at that
moment I

Know that you hear
I know that you feel
And I know that you care.

LOVE IS THIS

Giving instead of taking
Asking instead of demanding
Or doing just because

LOVE IS…
A friend to the friendless
An open ear during trials
And arms waiting to hold

LOVE IS…
A gentle kiss about the head
Caressing through the night
A call just to say I miss you

LOVE IS…
Enduring the storm
And knowing that your patience
Will get you over the mountain

LOVE IS…
Reaching the end of the rainbow
And finding you there

FRIENDS LIKE YOU

Friends like you are
hard to find, but
certainly worth the
search

HEAVEN

Though heaven is the place to be
I need to take the time
To see the wonders of the earth
So peaceful and sublime
Though angels speak about a place
Prepared for me to go
I need to feel the summer breeze
Embrace it as it blows
The majesty of you and me
To see the eagles fly
To see the seasons come and go
The beauty of the sky
The blessings of the gift of love
The days of joyful bliss
Are made to be a joy to see
A tragedy to miss
Though heaven is the place to be
I think I want to stay
Behold the sun and have a run
For just another day

SENSES

I hear the laughter of the sun
The singing of the rain
The glitter of the moon at night
The tapping on my pane

I see the flowers coming up
The budding of the trees
The sprouting of the sweetest fruit
The working of the bees

And yet there is a silence deep
A yearning of the heart
The sadness and the vagueness when
The world won't take a part

Bewildered is my state of mind
The beauty not beheld
The music that is not adorn
The flowers you won't smell

The elements, the elegance
The senses given us
Are for the use of saying thanks
To God in whom we trust

So say it loud and say it proud
I thank you for the gift
To hear and see your great beauty
Which gives us all a lift

ELEMENTS

My children

Look to the clouds, there's sight
Listen to the wind, it whispers
Saturate the sun, it warms

And know this

In the clouds I'm ever present
Through the wind you can hear me
And the sun is my hug to warm
you
With the breeze as my kiss to kiss
you

Because of these elements
I am never away from you

Forever with you, mom

BECAUSE OF YOU

Because of you, I have over come, for you made my mountain a molehill.

AN ANGEL CAME

An angel came to be with me
An angel came to soothe
An angel pulled me very close
And said, "It's time to move."

An angel heard my very cry
An angel felt my pain
An angel read my inner thoughts
Of how I felt insane

The deepest thoughts of loneliness
The struggles to reside
Within a world of carelessness
The need to surely hide

A hand extended from the north
And quickly traveled south
In minutes took away my stress
In minutes pulled me out

An angel came to be with me
An angel from above
An angel whispered in my ear
I'm here because of love.

IT'S MAGICAL

It's magical it's mystical
The way you make me sing
The way you make me laugh aloud
The happiness you bring

It's wonderful it's beautiful
The cheerfulness in store
I never know what is to come
And yet, I want it more

The walks upon a crowed beach
The movies after dark
The dinners by the candlelight
And strolls throughout the park

I can't explain and won't contain
Emotions through and through
Delightfulness a daily bliss
I get it all from you

It's magical it's mystical
With words I can't explain
I only know you cannot go
With me you must remain

MY SHELL

The hardness of my outer shell
The firmness of my heart
The distance that I had to have
No one could see a part
Of anything to do with me
I kept me to myself
And so alone, me on my own
I shared with no one else

And yet you broke the outer layer
To get inside of me
You softened up my harden soul
You took the time to see
That I was but a hurting girl
A victim of my past
A mourner living yesterday
Allowing it to last

You gathered up my every wrong
And gave to me the right
To live again from deep within
To dance in the moonlight
The words I need to say to you
I cannot say them well
No longer blue because of you
For breaking up my shell

BAD LUCK CUPID

If I could do one great thing
I could receive my other wing
For without two I cannot fly
Gracefully across the sky

Therefore my leader deemed a quest
And if by chance I pass the test
I'll be called like others, Cupid
But presently, they call me stupid

Now the challenge to be done
Is turning two into one
Bringing two forever close
Just one aim the perfect dose

There's the target here's the part
The arrow's headed for the heart
Oops, oh no I've missed again
It's not the heart I hit the chin

On second thought
Although it's sad
A one-wing back
Is not so bad

IN TIME

In time I've seen the ups and downs
The stand after the fall
In time I've seen the good and bad
I think I've seen it all

In time I've had the very best
In time I've had some hurt
I've cried a tear from year to year
But surely it was worth

The walks upon the whitest sand
The glance at every star
The setting moon and rising
Though memories are far

A subtle kiss upon my cheek
The stroking of my hair
A soft embrace and face to face
Into my eyes you'd stare

In time I know I'll have again
The warmth, the love, the glee
The very thing you used to bring
When you were next to me

In time,
I'll have it all in time

DEAR LORD

P.R.A.Y.

Promise
Revealing
Another
Yes

IF YOU COULD SEE

If you could see the you I do
The happiness the bliss
The radiation out from you
The joy that you remise

If you could know the things I do
The warmness that you give
The breath of life you seem to have
Allows me so to live

A mile is but a step or two
A mountain's not too high
A valley is the smallest dip
And you're the reason why

I count the blessings, not the tears
My weeping days are done
Unless they are the tears of joy
You've given everyone

If you could see the things I see
If you could know the view
Then you would know my inner glow
Is all because of you

STILL BE

If the sun never rose again,
My skin would still be warm.

If the rain refused to fall,
My thirst would still be quenched.

And if the moon sadly chose not to
dance with the stars,
There'd still be rhythm for me.

Because of you
All three would still be

THE DAY

Awaken by the morning rise
Out of the deepest sleep
To find the promise made to me
Again I did not keep

A pounding head as if the drums
Were beating to a song
A drink or two, then three and four
To drown out what was wrong

Another day of vision blurred
And memories unclear
Of what I did the night before
And whom I let in here

Reluctantly I turned my head
To see what I could see
I knew the answer all along
Again, how could it be?

An empty bottle on the desk
An empty soul inside
An empty home an empty life
The liquor helped to hide

The loneliness that I would feel
With every waking day
I used the drinks to dull the pain
To take it all away

As a magician on the stage
I used such trickery
I fooled them all, but in the end
The fool was really me

I'm praying for the day to come
I want so much to hold her
I know it's coming soon for me
The day I'll wake up sober

A BASEBALL DREAM

My season is here the best of them all
I've got a new bat to swing at the ball
I'm going to hit it, I know that I will
I'll run a few bases, another I'll steal

The pitcher is ready it's time to go up
In moment's I'll claim my victory cup
Here comes the pitch, there goes the swing
Around all the bases, I'll go with a zing

First base, second, base, third base, run
The most valued player, I know I'm the one
I made it to home, but ump didn't wait
To call me out for not touching the plate

But things worked out
For the best it seems
'Cause the only games won
Are the ones in my dreams

TO LOVE

If I've healed a hurt
Solaced a sigh
Caressed and kissed
In times of goodbye

I've cared

If I've held a hand
Or sang a song
Embraced, erased
A night too long

I've shared

If I've loved for life
The one I chose
From deepest depths
Our love arose

I've dared, I've shared, and cared

To love

TIME

A moment to become
A lifetime to be done

Time

A moment to reflect
A lifetime to forget

Time

A moment to behold
A lifetime growing old

Time

All I need is Time

THIS TREE

Our love is as deep
as the roots of this
tree,
Ever I love you
Ever you love
me

DEEPER THOUGHT

A deeper thoughts a deeper trance
I want you for a while
Think upon forgotten thoughts
The ones, which made you smile

A deeper thought a deeper trance
Remember once again
Yesterday, not far away
The memories of friends

Then say a word, a simple word
A phrase or even more
The tears from laugh, the times you had
For once, unlock the door

A deeper thought, a quote of old
Or maybe one of new
The words of wise, all truth, no lies
Are spoken just for you

A DEEPER THOUGHT

BE NOT

Be not the bloom, which bloomed too soon
And so, did not survive
Be not the bird, who flew too soon
And now is not alive

Be not the man, who could not see
Yet struggled hard to do
Be not the bloom, be not the bird,
Be not the man, be you

LOVE IS...

Love is not spoken, but deeply felt
Love is so strong and never melts

Love is a passion, a longing desire
A flashing flame, a roaring fire

Love is an itch, it can't be scratched
Love is a kingdom, it can't be matched

And though the intensions are very clear
Love takes control, in spite all of fear

So scream, and yell, and bellow out no
Love is a river and ever it flows

MY HEART

Everyday
I have to say
It's your romance
Which makes me dance

And as we dance
Into the dark
I ask for you
To take my heart

And every night
It's only right
For us to dare
A love to share

So have romance
To take a chance
Ignite a spark
And keep my heart

R.O.O.T

(Proverbs 12:3)

Results
Of
Occasional
Tests

you

I miss you most
When the summer moon is full
The winter nights are cold
When all my days grow long

I need you most
When trouble's on my mind
Peace is not at hand
When friends have failed again

I feel you most
When the wind whistles at my neck
The warm air wraps around me
When the breeze takes me away

And I cry the most
When I wake up and see
The lonely days ahead
When pain is hear again!

I MISS YOU MOST

REFLECTIONS

If by chance you see me
In silence, I'm not sad,
Yet reflecting on the
Joy you've give to me

G.L.O.W.

GIFT TO SHINE
LOVE THAT'S MINE
OPEN ARMS
WONDEROUS CHARM

GLOW,
YOU SIMPLY GLOW

I WISH (in memory of your loved one)

I wish that I could be the one
To fill your empty space
I wish that I could be the hand
To dry your weeping face

I wish that I could be the one
To carry such a load
I wish that I could be the one
To travel on your road

But if I took your status now
The pain that's in your heart
The void that is surrounding you
You'd never be a part

Of seeing Jesus at His best
At seeing Him become
The healer of your broken heart
The gift from God, the Son

You'd never know He's crying too
You'd never know He cares
You'd never cry for Him to help
You'd never know He's there

But I will be the one to pray
The one to ask the Lord
To bring you to a calming state
And give you your reward

And I will be the one who's here
Awaiting for your call
And I will be the earthly friend
To help you through it all

THE PERFECT D. R. U. G.

$\mathcal{D}$ELIVERING

$\mathcal{R}$ELIEVING

$\mathcal{U}$NDERSTANDING

$\mathcal{G}$OD

I LOVE YOU

I love you
From the height of your spirit
To the depth of your soul

I love you
From your every wrong
To your every right

I love you
In the softness of love
And the hardness of pain

I love you
And in all my dreams, hopes, and
Desires, I conclude, you must certainly
Love me too

Silence

If silence were to capture me
I know that it would find
A memory of you and me
In once upon a time
And yesterday not far away
Would live out once again
The finding of a chanted love
That time could never end
To reminisce of tenderness
Is thrilling, none the less
It can't behold the story told
Of heaven, how she blessed

Down upon the earth it came
The showers of the sky
A day or two then me and you
Told loneliness goodbye
Long ago or once upon
Oh, how the tale would start
Pulitzer prize from passing eyes
A love as fine as art
So here we are from yesterday
The present now at hand
And as we go it's sure to grow
A love destine to stand
If silence were to capture me
She'd listen as I say
Yes I do to me and you
Forever and a day

If I love you

If I love you today
I will love you tomorrow
When I give all I have
Not give I in sorrow
When 'morrow shall pass
Not pass thee my love
So quenching as water
Which falls from above
And sprouting will come
As blossoms from ground
First hide and then seek
New love we have found
If I love you today
I will love you tomorrow
For all I will give
No need shall you borrow

NOW I DO

Now that I love me
I can love you

Now that I need me
I will need you

Now that I cherish me
I do cherish you

Now, oh now

I can
I will
I do

POETIC B'S
(Mt. 5:3-12)

Blessed are the poor
The Kingdom is theirs
Blessed are the mourners
They know that He cares
Blessed are the seekers
Who look for a meal
The thirsty shall drink
And blessed to be filled
Blessed those of mercy
So much they'll obtain
Blessed are the pure
His sight they shall gain
Blessed are the peaceful
They're children of God
Blessed are the tortured
Their Kingdom, His rod
And blessed you accused
For me and my sake
The heaven I give
And sorrow I'll take

CHRIST

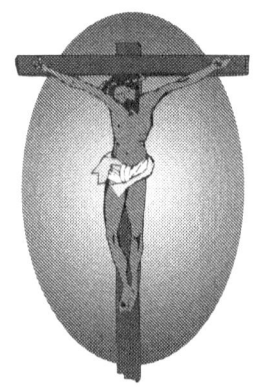

BORN: To reunite

Died: For our sins

Arose: To send the
          Comforter

ENDLESS

Twinkling stars
Grains of sands
Dates in cars
Hand and hand

Endless

Summer breeze
Skies of blue
Sunday ease
Me and you

Endless

Winters cold
Flowers bright
Hearts of gold
Day and night
Endless
We're simply

Endless

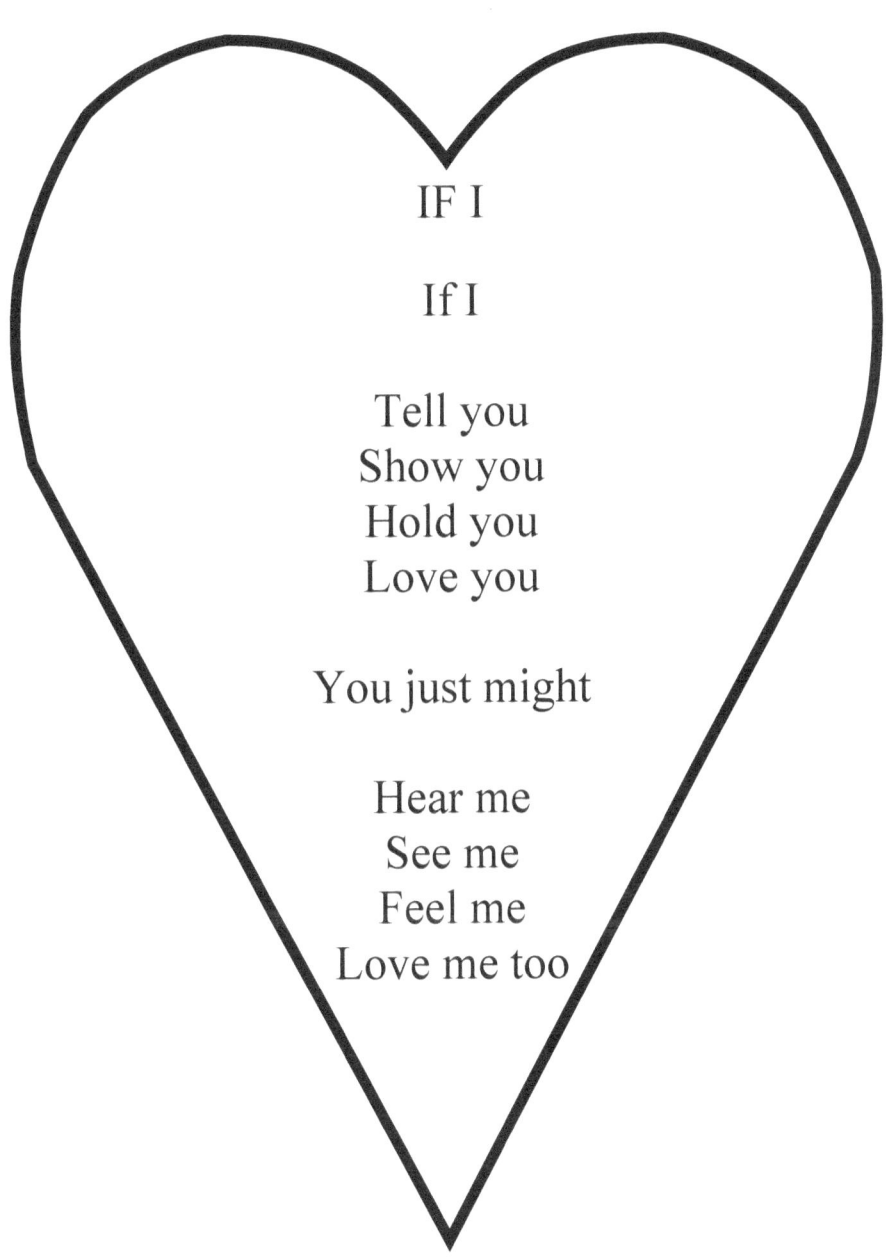

IF I

If I

Tell you
Show you
Hold you
Love you

You just might

Hear me
See me
Feel me
Love me too

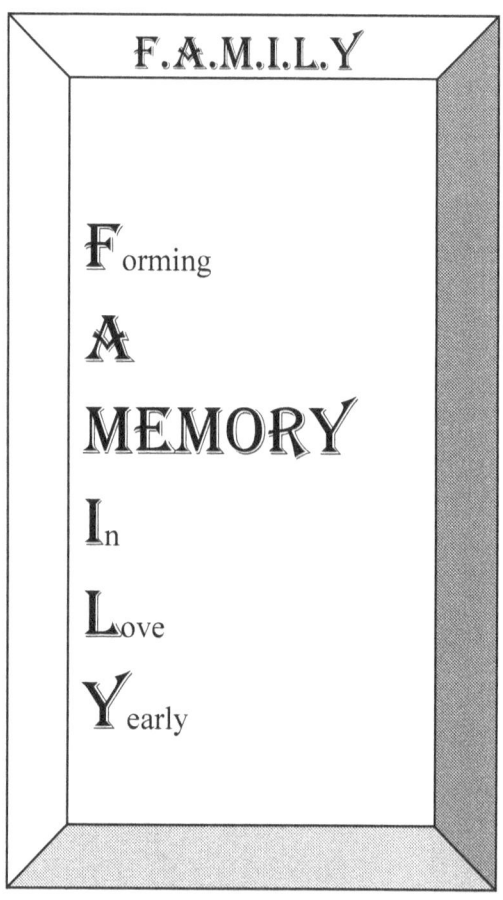

F.A.M.I.L.Y

Forming

A

MEMORY

In

Love

Yearly

L.O.V.E

Living

Out

Vibrant

Embraces

DREAM

The last thought
to cross my
mind before I
bed down, is the
thought of you.
Therefore, I'm
assured to have
a heavenly
dream

TWENTY-FIVE

Twenty-five is for silver
Fifty is for gold
But endless are the days
Our friendship will
behold

IT TAKES A FRIEND

It takes a friend to bring a smile
When things are going wrong
It takes a friend to walk a mile
To help you to be strong

It takes a friend to open up
To give a helping hand
To lend an ear and cry a tear
To say I understand

You are the one the warming sun
The shelter from the cold
The shining star that's never far
With you they broke the mold

Not only do you speak the truth
You speak it from within
As Mother Earth, you heal the hurt
And make me laugh again

It takes a friend I say again
To share a gift that's true
When you're around, I'm never down
I see the best in you

A DAY WITHOUT

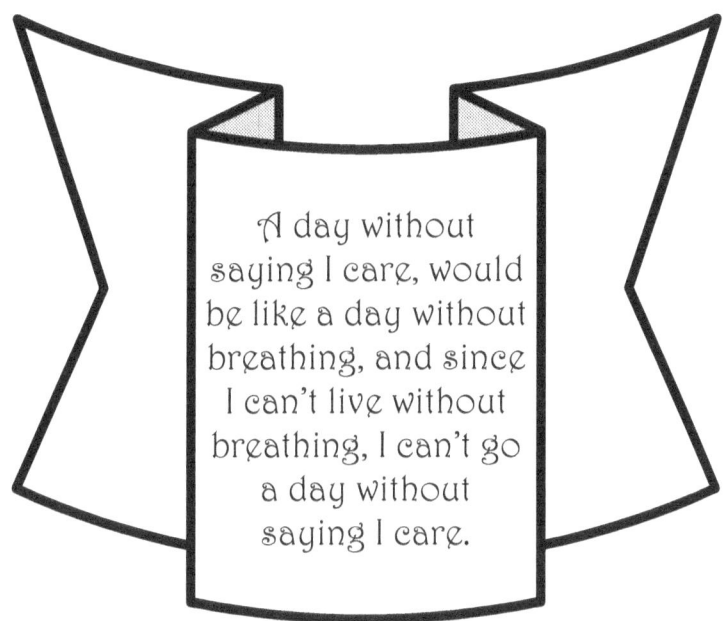

A day without saying I care, would be like a day without breathing, and since I can't live without breathing, I can't go a day without saying I care.

REMAIN

A sea of tears I'd surely cry
If one day you were gone
And sleepless nights would enter in
To meet the coming dawn

Oh I would ask a million times
From why, to when, and where
And I would search eternity
To find an answer there

But life is kind and I do find
Your tenderness and touch
Close to me to feel and see
Caress, to kiss, and such

Bestow, bestow, but do not go
Make not reality
The losing of your needed love
Remain a part of me

I'VE CRIED

I've cried about the prayers prayed
The wants and many needs
I've waited for the longest time
But did so not with ease

I've doubted every waking day
Suspecting in the end
That no would be the answer to
My prayers once again

But yet you looked beyond my doubts
Returning heaven's grace
Restoring all while giving more
To one who'd lost her faith

A nick of time the very thing
I needed came to be
A peace of mind, a calming time
An answer just for me

You came before I dropped my head
To cry another tear
A chime, the wind, it's you again
To prove you're always here

I have it now, I see it now
The no, I know, will pass
It's followed by the greatest yes
You save the best for last

DUTY

My duty is to forgive,
His grace helps me to
forget.

PLANTING

The planting of a friendship will spring into forever

I'VE NEVER

I've never won the lottery
I've never been of wealth
I've played the game the best I could
No matter what was dealt

I've never sailed the seven seas
I've never been to France
I'm not compared to beauty queens
And yet, I've had the chance

To smell the blossom of a rose
To saturate the sun
To wrestle in the whitest snow
And do it just for fun

To stroll across the widest beach
To hold the strongest hand
To bare my deepest, inner thoughts
To hear, "I understand."

For after all these are the things
We cherish and behold
A summer love like hand and glove
Until the days of old

And though I may not have it all
I know I'll never say
I've never had the gift of love
It's with me everyday

S E A S O N S

The autumn leaves have fallen
With the winter on its way
The birds I hear them calling
We'll sing another day
The morning rise is slow
With the night upon us soon
The stars are still aglow
And there's beauty in the moon
The rain turns into snow
As the heat turns into cold
But happy I am though
For it's you I have to hold
At last I now can say
That I've found my love so true
'Cause nightly I did pray
And God answered me with you
So winter take your time
Bringing all you have to bring
For love is the reason
I'll have another spring

THE NIGHT

A silent night a peaceful night
Of rest one can endure
Angelic thoughts to rest the mind
The night safe and secure

But now with you away so long
The night becomes the beast
Screams and yells to shake my soul
Unnerving at the least

How can I calm the spirits wild
How can I bid them gone
When miles away you are from me
The nights forever longs

Shadows creep out from the walls
The ceiling and the floor,
Cannot save me from the night
I call for you once more

Until the time when you are here
The night will always be
The ghost that haunts me all night long
So night can't set me free

AFTER

After night there is the day
After morning there is dew
After sunshine there is light
After old there is the new

After what has come to be
After sorrow's had its way
After all the tears have fallen
After pain, a brighter day

After winter comes the spring
After spring we surely know
Is the joy of the summer
The warmth won't let you go

After all the changing seasons
After poets end their rhyme
After all is said and done
I will help you through this time

After crying there is laughter
From below there is above
After presence there is absence
But forever there is love

I SEE

I see laughter through the pain
Sunshine over rain
Summer in the snow
A yes instead of no

I see

I see rivers from the streams
The promise from my dreams
The ups and never downs
The smiles instead of frowns

I see

I see flowers from a seed
A hand given in need
A life that's never board
The wonders of the Lord

I see

I SIMPLY CHOOSE TO SEE

YOU

You walked with me
And talked with me
Took strides with me
And cried with me

You

You stayed with me
And prayed with me
Looked into me
And took from me

You

You chanced with me
And danced with me
Lived with me
To give to me

You

IT'S ALL BECAUSE OF YOU

I FEAR

I fear the time will never come
For all of us to live
Walking, talking, side by side,
A joyful love to give

I fear that I will never see
That she, and he, and I
Will be a rainbow blending with
The robins in the sky

For every wrong there is a right
To take away the pain
Until mistreatment rise again
To override the gain

I fear the dream that Martin had
Will never come to be
Boys and girls, blue jeans and curls
Just playing happily

I fear this nation will not see
That it would be worthwhile
To change the past and make it last
So everyone may smile

Loved ones

To all my precious loved ones
I'm missed I know it's true
And if given but a moment
I'd say I miss you too

But the glory of the Lord
With all His given grace
Would want you all to know
I'm in a better place

I know your hearts are heavy
And I know you want to cry
But do you know our Father
Did not let me die?

So for a moment miss me
And for a moment weep
But know within yourselves
For a moment I'm asleep

Just know that I'm in comfort
And this is not the end
For he has promised me
I'll see you all again

Thank You

Thank you for this moment spent
To share your time with me
To read a line, upon a time
My words poetically

And thank you for the treasured space
Invaded by my gift
And in return I hope I've earned
The chance to give a lift

Raise oh spirit from within
Embrace my readers tight
Soothe them as a lullaby
And turn their wrong to right

Thank you for this moment spent
To share my gift and thought
And thank you for supporting me
Such happiness you've brought

www.ingramcontent.com/pod-product-compliance
Lightning Source LLC
Chambersburg PA
CBHW030357290526
45785CB00004B/1799